Superstars of Wrestling
"THE AMERICAN NIGHTMARE" CODY

BY BENJAMIN PROUDFIT

Gareth Stevens
PUBLISHING

Please visit our website, www.garethstevens.com. For a free color catalog of all our high-quality books, call toll free 1-800-542-2595 or fax 1-877-542-2596.

Library of Congress Cataloging-in-Publication Data

Names: Proudfit, Benjamin, author.
Title: "The American nightmare" Cody / Benjamin Proudfit.
Other titles: The American nightmare Cody
Description: New York : Gareth Stevens Publishing, [2022] | Series: Superstars of wrestling | Includes index.
Identifiers: LCCN 2020032239 (print) | LCCN 2020032240 (ebook) | ISBN 9781538265833 (library binding) | ISBN 9781538265819 (paperback) | ISBN 9781538265826 (set) | ISBN 9781538265840 (ebook)
Subjects: LCSH: Rhodes, Cody, 1985---Juvenile literature. | Wrestlers--United States--Biography--Juvenile literature. | Wrestling--Juvenile literature. | World Wrestling Entertainment, Inc.--Juvenile literature.
Classification: LCC GV1196.R86 P76 2022 (print) | LCC GV1196.R86 (ebook) | DDC 796.812092 [B]--dc23
LC record available at https://lccn.loc.gov/2020032239
LC ebook record available at https://lccn.loc.gov/2020032240

First Edition

Published in 2022 by
Gareth Stevens Publishing
111 East 14th Street, Suite 349
New York, NY 10003

Copyright © 2022 Gareth Stevens Publishing

Designer: Michael Flynn
Editor: Kristen Nelson

Photo credits: Cover, pp. 1, 7 Icon Sport/Getty Images; p. 5 (Cody Rhodes) Michael N. Todaro/Getty Images; p. 5 (Dusty Rhodes) Moses Robinson/Getty Images; p. 9 Simon Hofmann/Bongarts/Getty Images; p. 11 Ethan Miller/Getty Images; p. 13 George Napolitano/FilmMagic/Getty Images; p. 15 Mike Coppola/Getty Images; p. 17 Jeff Kravitz/FilmMagic/Getty Images; p. 19 https://commons.wikimedia.org/wiki/File:Cody_Rhodes_ROH_World_Champion.jpg; p. 21 George Napolitano/MediaPunch/IPX/AP Images; p. 23 Presley Ann/Getty Images; p. 25 Joe Seer/Shutterstock.com; p. 27 Emma McIntyre/Getty Images; p. 29 Paras Griffin/Getty Images.

All rights reserved. No part of this book may be reproduced in any form without permission in writing from the publisher, except by a reviewer.

Printed in the United States of America

CPSIA compliance information: Batch #CSGS22: For further information contact Gareth Stevens, New York, New York at 1-800-542-2595.

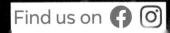

CONTENTS

Family Business	4
Big Debut	8
Tag Team Champ!	10
Out on His Own	16
Going All In	20
The Start of AEW	22
Into the Future	28
The Best of Cody	30
For More Information	31
Glossary	32
Index	32

FAMILY BUSINESS

"The American Nightmare" Cody has always been bound for **professional** wrestling greatness. He was born in Georgia on June 30, 1985, as Cody Runnels, the son of Michelle Runnels and wrestling **legend** Dusty Rhodes. He has three siblings: Dustin, Kristin, and Teil.

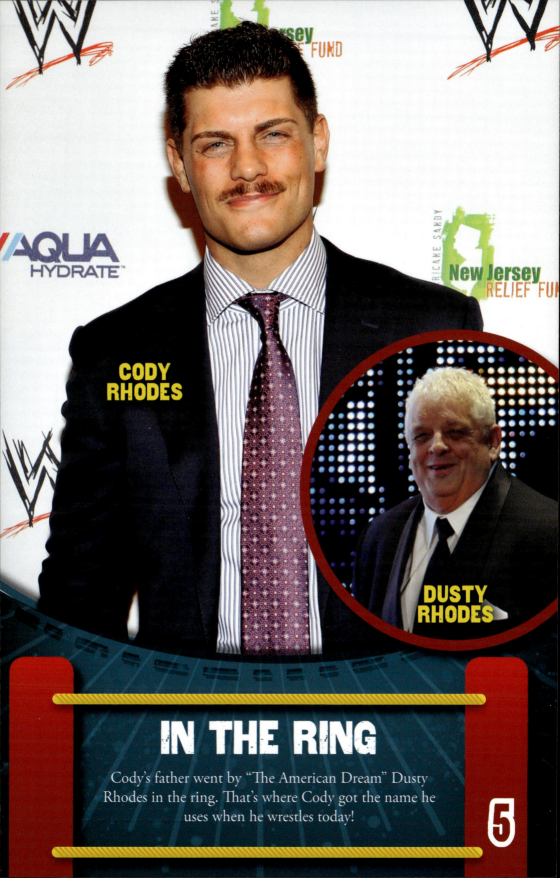

IN THE RING

Cody's father went by "The American Dream" Dusty Rhodes in the ring. That's where Cody got the name he uses when he wrestles today!

In high school in Marietta, Georgia, Cody was an **amateur** wrestler. He won the Georgia State Championship in the 189-pound (85.7 kg) weight class in 2003 and 2004. Soon after high school, he started training in the ring for professional wrestling.

IN THE RING

Cody started using the name Cody Rhodes as a teenager. However, his first in-ring name was Cody Runnels.

BIG DEBUT

In 2006, Cody started wrestling in Ohio Valley Wrestling, a **developmental** part of World Wrestling Entertainment (WWE). He wasn't there long. In July 2007, Cody **debuted** on *Monday Night Raw*. His first match was against Randy Orton.

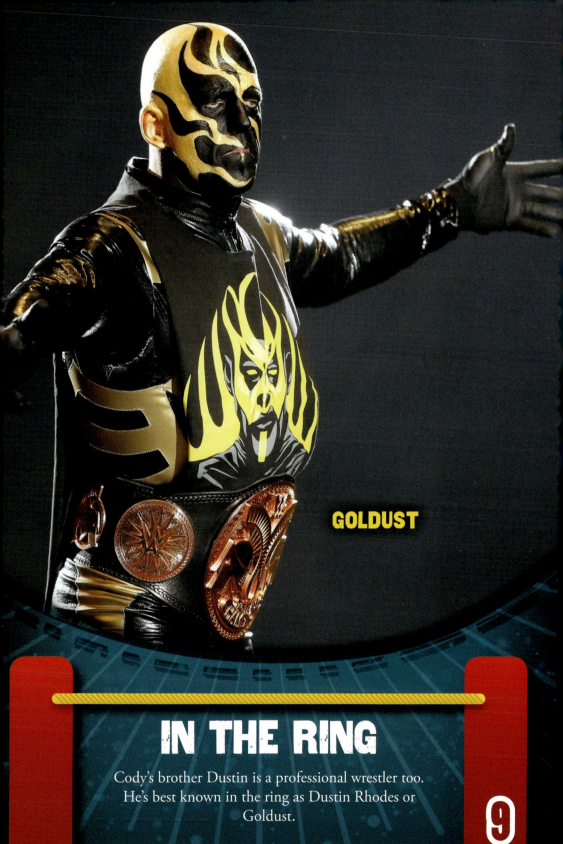

GOLDUST

IN THE RING

Cody's brother Dustin is a professional wrestler too. He's best known in the ring as Dustin Rhodes or Goldust.

TAG TEAM CHAMP!

Cody went on to become a tag team champion, first with Hardcore Holly and then with Ted DiBiase Jr. He and Ted linked up with Randy Orton to create the Legacy, as all three of them came from families known for pro wrestling.

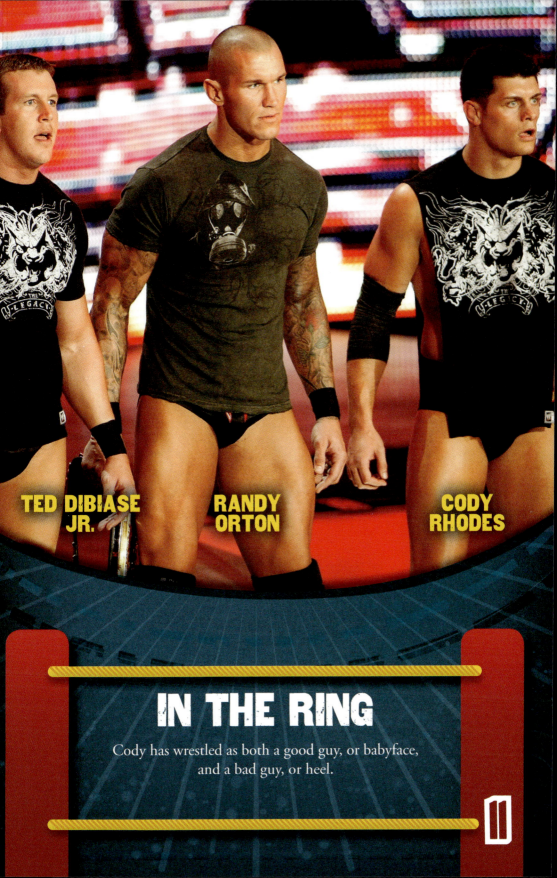

TED DIBIASE JR.   **RANDY ORTON**   **CODY RHODES**

IN THE RING

Cody has wrestled as both a good guy, or babyface, and a bad guy, or heel.

In 2010, Cody moved to the WWE show *SmackDown*. He became a tag team champion again with Drew McIntyre at Night of Champions. A **feud** with Rey Mysterio then led him to win a match at WrestleMania 27 in April 2011!

IN THE RING

In August 2011, Cody won the WWE Intercontinental Championship. He lost it to the Big Show at WrestleMania 28 in April 2012.

By 2013, Cody again found himself as part of a tag team. This time he was paired with his brother as Goldust. The following year, he debuted as Stardust. The next few years were hard for Cody, who felt stuck wrestling as Stardust.

BRANDI RHODES

IN THE RING

Cody married his wife Brandi in 2013. She was a ring announcer called Eden for WWE. As a pro wrestler, she goes by Brandi Rhodes.

OUT ON HIS OWN

Cody left the WWE in May 2016. He began wrestling with top **independent** companies like Ring of Honor (ROH) and Total Nonstop Action Wrestling (now Impact Wrestling). He was seen as changing how pro wrestling had worked for many years.

THE YOUNG BUCKS

KENNY OMEGA

IN THE RING

Cody posted a list of wrestlers he wanted to work with after he left WWE. It included Kurt Angle, Adam Cole, the Young Bucks, and Roderick Strong.

In 2017, Cody won the ROH World Championship. He also debuted with New Japan Pro Wrestling (NJPW) as part of the Bullet Club, alongside the Young Bucks, Matt and Nick Jackson. Cody and the Jacksons soon planned a wrestling show—a big one.

IN THE RING

The Young Bucks are part of a popular YouTube channel called Being the Elite with Kenny Omega and often featuring Cody.

GOING ALL IN

Cody and the Young Bucks were told they couldn't sell 10,000 tickets to an independent wrestling show. But they did! All In took place in Chicago, Illinois, on September 1, 2018. Cody won the NWA Heavyweight Championship, a title his father had held.

IN THE RING

All In sold out in under half an hour!

THE START OF AEW

The success of All In led to Cody's next step with the Young Bucks: their own wrestling company. At the start of 2019, the launch of All Elite Wrestling (AEW) was announced on the Being the Elite YouTube channel.

AEW WRESTLING

IN THE RING

Cody is an executive vice president of AEW. His wife Brandi is the chief brand officer.

AEW's first big show was Double or Nothing in May 2019. Cody took on his brother Dustin and won! Cody won again at All Out in September in a match against Shawn Spears. About a month later, AEW debuted on TV!

IN THE RING

Cody told *Sports Illustrated* in 2016: "I didn't leave WWE to prove them wrong, but it sure … feels good when I do."

25

In April 2020, Cody took part in an eight-man **tournament** for the TNT Championship. Cody beat Shawn Spears and Darby Allin to make it to the finals at Double or Nothing in May. He won the title against Lance Archer.

IN THE RING

Cody became the first ever TNT Champion in AEW.

INTO THE FUTURE

Cody is a great in-ring wrestler as well as someone who wants to make the wrestling business better. His work is bringing some of the best wrestlers in the world to AEW! There's no doubt Cody is creating a legend of his own.

IN THE RING

Even though Cody is succeeding on his own, he won't say he's never going back to the WWE!

29

THE BEST OF CODY

SIGNATURE MOVES
Alabama slam, disaster kick

FINISHERS
cross Rhodes, American nightmare

ACCOMPLISHMENTS
WWE Tag Team Champion
WWE Intercontinental Champion
Ring of Honor World Champion
IWGP U.S. Champion
AEW TNT Champion

MATCHES TO WATCH
2017 NJPW G1 Special in the USA
vs. Kazuchika Okada; 2018 ROH
Supercard of Honor XII vs. Kenny
Omega; 2020 AEW Double or
Nothing vs. Dustin Rhodes

FOR MORE INFORMATION

BOOKS

Abdo, Kenny. *Pro Wrestling*. Minneapolis, MN: Fly!, an Imprint of Abdo Zoom, 2019.

Black, Jake. *WWE Ultimate Superstar Guide*. New York, NY: DK | Penguin Random House, 2018.

WEBSITES

AEW | All Elite Wrestling Roster
www.allelitewrestling.com/roster
Check out the other wrestlers Cody works with on AEW's website.

All Elite Wrestling | Bleacher Report
bleacherreport.com/all-elite-wrestling
Follow along with what happens each week on the AEW tab of Bleacher Report.

Publisher's note to educators and parents: Our editors have carefully reviewed these websites to ensure that they are suitable for students. Many websites change frequently, however, and we cannot guarantee that a site's future contents will continue to meet our high standards of quality and educational value. Be advised that students should be closely supervised whenever they access the internet.

GLOSSARY

amateur: having to do with the kind of wrestling done on school teams and in the Olympics

debut: to make a first appearance

developmental: having to do with the growth of something or someone

feud: a long fight between two people

independent: not owned by a larger business

legend: a famous person known for doing something very well

professional: earning money from an activity that many people do for fun

tournament: a sports contest that many teams or people take part in over the course of many days

INDEX

All Elite Wrestling (AEW) 22, 23, 24, 26, 28

All In 20, 21, 22

Being the Elite 18, 22

DiBiase, Ted Jr. 10, 11

Monday Night Raw 8

Omega, Kenny 17, 18

Orton, Randy 8, 10, 11

Rhodes, Brandi 15, 23

Rhodes, Dustin 4, 9, 14, 24

Rhodes, Dusty 4, 5

Ring of Honor (ROH) 16, 18

SmackDown 12

World Wrestling Entertainment (WWE) 8, 12, 15, 16, 17, 25, 29

WrestleMania 12

Young Bucks 17, 18, 20, 22